Lakeland
Fifty Years Ago

Lakeland
Fifty Years Ago

by

Kenneth Shepherd

Introduction by A.Wainwright

WG

Westmorland Gazette, Kendal, Cumbria

First Published 1989

ISBN 0 902272 79 9

Published by
Westmorland Gazette,
22 Stricklandgate, Kendal, Cumbria LA9 4NE

Printed by
Dixon Printing Co. Ltd., Kendal, Cumbria

Introduction

Ken Shepherd has been a commentator of the Lakeland scene for over half a century, his medium of expression being the lens of his camera. His particular interest in the early years was to portray in pictures the everyday life of the dalesfolk who at that time were insular communities in a favoured environment of natural beauty undisturbed by the pressures of the world outside. Lakeland then was a sanctuary of profound peace and rural tranquillity. Ken's photographs were evocative of the romantic atmosphere of the region.

He commenced his career in the photographic department of the Westmorland Gazette in Kendal, later joining the Carlisle Journal as staff photographer, his work there being interrupted by four and a half years service in the Fleet Air Arm, after which he returned to civilian life in Kendal as a freelance photographer. His professional skills were soon to receive wide acclaim and he received commissions from national periodicals and publishers of illustrated magazines, calendars and view cards, while his services became increasingly in demand locally at social and civic occasions. There are many homes and institutions in the district that proudly display framed pictures bearing the signature 'Kenneth Shepherd, Kendal', and they are much treasured.

He retired from the public limelight and ceased his activities some ten years ago, and it was only by chance that I discovered in a recent conversation that he had retained and preserved the prints and negatives of his early pictures taken in the 1930s and 1940s. When I asked to see them he produced a selection of such outstanding merit and beauty of composition that I felt they should not linger in obscurity; moreover they recalled to mind the Lakeland I once knew so well when it was a sanctuary of peace before the postwar influx of tourists and their cars and coaches and caravans drained away the charm of the villages and valleys.

The Gazette, equally delighted, needed no persuasion to reproduce these early photographs in this book. They have given me much pleasure, bringing vividly back to mind happy memories, now growing dim, of the Lakeland I once knew well and loved for its quiet beauty. This book will, I am sure, give great joy to others, especially those contemporary with the times of the illustrations. Ken's pictures tell us of an era of Lakeland that has gone and is almost forgotten. They give new life to fading memories.

To
Winnie, Ian and Rosemary

Author's Note

Fifty years have elapsed since the first of these photographs was taken. They have lain undisturbed until, by chance, I mentioned their existance to my good friend Alfred Wainwright whose enthusiasm persuaded me to consider publishing them. However, the passing of time had erased many details from my memory and, in order to confirm names and location details, I once again contacted the folk and their descendants who had so graciously posed for me all those years ago. If, therefore, one or two small errors still exist, I trust that readers will overlook the frailties of advanced age and the consequent deterioration of memory.

My researches have taken me to many remote areas of the Lake District where I have been received with the utmost kindness and generosity. Cumbrian folk are renowned for their hospitality and my appreciation of their time and interest is gratefully acknowledged. I also wish to include a tribute to the late Jim Cookson; several of his photographs are included in this volume, the copyright of which was passed to me by his family. I must also record my thanks to Titus Wilson & Son Limited of Kendal who kindly gave permission to quote from Bruce L. Thompson's book 'The Lake District and The National Trust' published in 1946.

Most of the photographs are from glass plate negatives and were taken on a variety of cameras, the earliest of which was a Goerz Anschutz Press Camera (5" x 4"). I also used a Dallmeyer Single Lens Reflex Camera ($4^1/_4$" x $3^1/_4$"), a Voigtländer Camera ($3^1/_4$" x $2^1/_4$") and an Agfa Folding Film Camera ($3^1/_4$" x $2^1/_4$").

Kenneth Shepherd

The Jaws of Borrowdale

This stretch of the River Derwent (or Oak River) is fordable on only a few days each year. The heavy rain that falls on the converging valleys of Seathwaite, Seatoller and Stonethwaite quickly causes flooding in the Jaws of Borrowdale.

The photograph shows a cart belonging to Hollows Farm below Maiden Moor crossing the ford to reach the main Keswick to Borrowdale road. In the background are the serrated tops of Rosthwaite Fell leading to Glaramara.

The Cobbler of Nether Bridge

John Richardson outside his cobbler's shop, one of the Glebe Cottages beside Nether Bridge in Kirkland, Kendal. He was so fond of flowers that he planted nasturtiums in old, worn-out boots, which also advertised his trade.

He had previously worked at the K Shoe Factory as a hand-stitch man. After the introduction of time clocks he left his job and set up a cobbler's shop. His price for soling and heeling a pair of ladies shoes was 2s. 6d.; the cost for mens' shoes was 4s. 9d. Hand sewing was 6d. extra.

He was rarely seen without his clay pipe in which he smoked black twist and would proudly tell everyone that he made the climbing boots worn by Dr. Wakefield for the 1922 expedition to Mount Everest.

Sadgill, Longsleddale

"A little scene of exquisite beauty surrounded by images of greatness".

Within the valley of Longsleddale, beside the River Sprint, lies the beautiful hamlet of Sadgill. Nestling at the base of Rough Crags and Goat Scar, this peaceful little settlement conveys an aura of tranquillity rarely found today.

Beyond the village, at the head of the valley, a track leads over Gatescarth Pass down into Mardale and Haweswater and is today much used by fellwalkers.

The owners of Sadgill Farm are related to the family which formerly occupied Hartrigg Farm in the neighbouring valley of Kentmere.

A 'Boon Do' at Hartrigg

A busy scene from the 1930s at Hartrigg Farm, near the head of Kentmere. Neighbouring farmers and their workers assist Mr. and Mrs. Fishwick to complete the annual sheep shearing. The men use hand clippers and standard clipping stools as can be seen in the photograph.

The gathering became known as a 'boon' clipping and, to celebrate its finish and to thank their neighbours, the farmer served a large meal in one of his barns.

Throughout Cumberland and Westmorland,'boon do's' were held at many farms for a variety of annual events, e.g. hedging, ploughing, etc. and the goodwill that these gatherings promoted within the farming community still exists today.

Harvesting Bracken on the Howgills

Deep in the Howgill Fells, high above Chapel Beck, two farm workers harvest bracken from the eastern slopes for use as bedding for the local cattle.

This mass of fells lying on the eastern fringes of Lakeland and little frequented by tourists, still retains a degree of remoteness that is so strikingly portrayed in the photograph.

A 'Canny Cummerlan' Lad

Many people today will remember the annual 'Cummerlan Neet' held in the Silver Grill Restaurant in English Street, Carlisle. Well known local Cumbrians gathered together for a meal of traditional Cumberland dishes and afterwards sat and reminisced about times now long forgotten.

The photograph is a study of one such son of Cumberland, a gentleman from the Caldbeck area. His face, so full of character, expresses a life of hard toil and simple pleasures.

In Old Hawkshead

The delightful village of Hawkshead has long been a favourite with visitors to the Lake District. Its uniqueness has thankfully remained untouched by modern developments.

The National Trust now owns a number of cottages in the village including the original office of Heelis Solicitors. William Heelis was the husband of Beatrix Potter who owned nearby Hill Top Farm in Near Sawrey. William Wordsworth's name is also connected with the history of Hawkshead; he attended the Grammar School that can still be found on the edge of the village.

Seen in the photograph are Mr. and Mrs. Joe Wright walking along Flag Street with a friend.

Townend, Troutbeck

Townend, Troutbeck was built in 1626 by George Browne, an 'independent statesman' and was until 1944 occupied for thirteen generations by the same family.

The Townend estate was transferred to the National Trust in 1947. Much work has been done by the Trust to restore the house and garden to represent a typical yeoman farmer's house in the county of Westmorland.

The barn on the opposite side of the road is a bank barn and is still used for agricultural purposes. Its gallery can clearly be seen in the photograph.

Westmorland's Abbey

Shap Abbey was founded by the Premonstratensian Canons in 1199. After the dissolution of
the monastries by Henry VIII in the sixteenth century, the abbey fell into disrepair. This romantic
ruin now stands as a lonely sentinel keeping watch over the adjacent moorland of Shap Fell,
guarding the sheep around its base.

The flock of ewes and their lambs in the photograph belong to the farm in the lee of the abbey
and has been managed by the Bindloss family for many years.

"There was Peace on Nether Bridge"

Mr. and Mrs. William Dobson of Sellet Hall near Stainton make their way homeward over the partly-cobbled surface of Nether Bridge after Market Day in Kendal.

The picture was taken in the early 1940s and captures the unhurried pace of life at that time.

'Lile Ratty'

The much loved Ravenglass and Eskdale Railway, known with affection as 'Lile Ratty', is one of the great attractions of Lakeland and carries thousands of passengers from Ravenglass along the beautiful valley of Eskdale to the terminus at Dalegarth.

Originally opened in 1875 to transport iron ore and stone from the Muncaster and Boot quarries to meet the Furness Railway at Ravenglass, this little line now carries only passenger traffic under the protection of the Ravenglass and Eskdale Railway Preservation Society.

The photograph, taken in 1948, shows 'The River Irt', one of the line's oldest locomotives, ready to use the turntable at Dalegarth before its return journey through Eskdale.

Turning Hay Beside Elter Water

A clear summer day in Lakeland and a welcome chance for Allan Wilson and his mother Sally of Tarn Foot Farm to gently turn the hay in the field beside Elter Water. Behind, the Langdale Pikes are mirrored in the stillness of the lake.

Spring Lambs Beneath the Damson Trees

The damson trees of the Lyth Valley near Kendal have been famous for generations. The spring blossom and the new season's lambs proclaim the end of winter and herald the arrival of warmer weather and longer days.

Unfortunately, some of the fruit trees are old and past their best. Their plums are difficult to pick and the branches are often left unharvested.

Debatable Afforestation

In about 1790 the Governors of Greenwich Hospital introduced Scots pines and larch into the Keswick area. Other residents around Windermere soon followed their example, causing concern among the local residents whose preference for indigenous plant species was voluably expressed.

Afforestation on a commercial basis was initiated by Manchester Corporation Waterworks Committee beside the shores of Thirlmere in the early part of this century. After the Second World War ended, a number of Forestry Commissioners were appointed and extensive forests were planted at Bassenthwaite, Whinlatter Pass and Ennerdale.

Much publicised opposition to afforestation has resulted in the creation of a joint committee comprising members of the Council for the Preservation of Rural England and The Forestry Commission to try and minimise the effects of large-scale planting on the environment.

The photograph shows the felling of immature trees for the Christmas season.

Joe Cowman of Eskdale

Joe Cowman was the tenant of two National Trust farms, Penny Hill and then Wha House, both in Upper Eskdale.

After the end of the Second World War, he and his wife Pat opened their farmhous to provide food and accommodation for a small number of visitors. The welcome they extended to their guests and their kindness is still remembered by many who enjoyed their hospitality.

Joe would often take his sheep up onto the open fell for me to photograph. The backdrop of Harter Fell and Upper Eskdale made these photographic sessions a delight.

In the Shadow of Helvellyn

A flock of Herdwick and Swaledale crossed ewes, recently clipped, fords Grisedale Beck near Patterdale, creating a photograph of perfect harmony.

Dominating the skyline are the rugged outlines of Dollywaggon Pike, Helvellyn and to the right Eagle Crag. The delightful track that follows the beck up the valley to its source in Grisedale Tarn snugly hugs the lower slopes of St. Sunday Crag, seen on the left of the picture.

"His Chosen Exile"

The familiar figure of Mr. J. Wearmouth of Eskdale. A native of the Northumberland coast, he left his home early in the 1940s to escape the bombardment of wartime Tyneside and settled in a wooden cabin near the village of Boot, below the looming mass of Ulpha Fell.

His stylised carvings of birds and animals from local wood were in great demand by early visitors.

"The Bridal of Triermain"

The entrance to the Vale of St. John near Keswick is dominated by a massive spur protruding from Watson's Dodd called Castle Rock.

This tree-clad outcrop is mentioned in the famous poem by Sir Walter Scott "The Bridal of Triermain" and is referred to locally as 'Triermain Rock'.

The Deepest Lake, The Highest Mountain

I spent Easter weekend in 1934 at Wasdale where snow still lingered on the very tops of the peaks overlooking England's deepest lake. Wastwater's beauty is aggressive and awesome but so often bad weather hides its frightening grandeur.

There were no other visitors to spoil the feeling of isolation apart from these three girls from West Cumberland who had come to explore the hidden treasures that this isolated valley so begrudgingly offers.

A Youngster's View of Eskdale

High on Keppel Crag by Birker Force, my young son Ian looks down on Eskdale, surely the loveliest and most unspoilt valley of Lakeland.

The newly-built youth hostel in the centre of the photograph was the forerunner of a series of such establishments which have enabled youngsters to discover for themselves the majesty of the mountains.

Eskdale is richly supplied with paths and bridleways that lead to the summits of the surrounding fells. Unfrequented Upper Eskdale offers access to subtler charms; the waterfalls of Throstle Garth, the solitude of Burnmoor Tarn and Devoke Water, and the beauty of Lingcove Beck.

The Unchanging Howgills

In peaceful solitude, Miles ('Miley') Airey of Lowgill Farm lays a hedge above the tiny hamlet of Beck Foot. Behind, the gently rounded tops of the Howgill Fells, still sprinkled with the remains of the last snowfall, stand proudly against the skyline.

Even in this remote area, man has left his mark; the impressive but obsolete viaduct once carried the branch railway line beside the beautiful River Lune from Lowgill to Sedbergh.

Davey Bank by The Crook O' Lune

This charming old farmhouse at Davey Bank lies in the shadow of the lonely Howgill Fells near to a loop of the River Lune known locally as The Crook o' Lune. The date on the porch reads 1755.

The Middleton family have farmed these eastern fringes of Westmorland for many generations. Even the nearby presence of the new M6 motorway has failed to disturb the stillness that permeates the dale.

The Old Mill

On the bank of the rushing beck, opposite the farm at Davey Bank, stands the old cornmill. The photograph shows George Alderson, the last worker at the mill, leading the horse over the stone bridge towards the farm. The cart contains sacks of milled corn that will be fed to the cattle during the long winters.

Although the building is still in existence, the mill was closed many years ago.

Haytime

Members of the Postlethwaite family of Riddings Farm, Howgill, together turn the hay on their land by the Fair Mile, a quiet road that skirts the foot of the Howgill Fells from Tebay to Sedbergh.

Mr. and Mrs. Postlethwaite work at the front and end of the line, their daughters Peggy and Betty and two farm helpers stand between. The dog quietly watches their labours.

A Peaceful Sunrise

In July 1946 the Kendal Methodist Church Youth Group organised a night climb up Helvellyn to celebrate the coming of peace at the end of World War Two.

Conscious that most visitors who climb the 3,118 feet to view the famous spectacle of the sun rising behind Fiend's Fell on Cross Fell endure the vigil only to see a blanket of mist and rain, we were privileged on that occasion to see a most glorious sunrise. The glowing rays highlighted the furthest reaches of Ullswater and illuminated the rivers and tarns of the intervening fells.

Celebrating his Ninetieth Birthday

Tobias Atkinson of Crosslands, Old Hutton spent most of his 90th birthday raking hay and, judging by the uniform lines of hay in the background, his great age had not impaired his ability.

The quietness of this secluded corner has in recent years been shattered by the continual roar of traffic on the nearby M6 motorway.

"**W**hile Barred Clouds Bloom the Soft Dying Day"
(John Keats)

The last gleam of the westering sun penetrates the patterned strath of Eskdale while the evening clouds bloom the spurs of the Scafells. Behind Wha House Farm, momentarily illuminated, the rocks of Hare Crag seem to be almost alive with inward light.

I photographed this glorious panorama one evening during the spring of 1948 when the gentle words of John Keats so accurately reflected the glory of the scene unfolding before me.

Only the View is Unchanged

The Pikes of Langdale and the bulk of Loughrigg Fell look across Windermere to a scene of unhurried tranquillity as a flock of Herdwick hoggs are moved to their winter pastures.

Few people today will recognise the location of this photograph. The development of the Water Ski Centre and the traffic congestion on the A591 road beside Low Wood Hotel make it impossible to retake this picture some forty years on.

Happy Days

A hot summer's day and a party of school girls enjoy the cool, quiet waters of Windermere. The post war years have seen a dramatic increase in the numbers of visitors to England's longest lake; rarely indeed do we now see the lake as peaceful as in the photograph.

In the background are the high fells of the Troutbeck Valley.

Character Studies at Kendal Auction Mart

Charles Medcalf of Bentham and Thomas Hutchinson of Browfoot, Burneside, compare notes at Kendal Auction Mart in June, 1939.

Friends at Kendal Auction Mart

Mr. T. Prickett of Barrows Green (left) and Mr. W. Dobson of Sellet Hall, Stainton, pause during the day's proceedings for a private conversation.

Kendal Auction Mart Officials

Mr. J.W. Hartley of Newhouse, Burneside (Head Director) and Mr. J. Ion of Kidside, Milnthorpe, discuss the day's transactions.

The Prize Show

Mr. E. Bindloss of Shap Abbey Farm and Mr. R. Cottam of Skelsmergh Hall judge a pen of grey faced hoggs at Kendal Auction Mart. Mr. Robinson of Preston Patrick (with the white beard) looks on.

A Bit of a Puzzle

Mr. J. Dargue of Burneside Hall in characteristic attitude at the Kendal Auction Mart. With him is Mr. J.R. Tomlinson of Common Mire, Endmoor.

The Wettest Place in England

The tiny hamlet of Seathwaite, at the end of the road from Keswick to Borrowdale, is well known as the wettest place in England. The average rainfall up to 1946 was 125.30 inches per year compared with 21.79 inches in London.

On 2nd November 1898 nearly 5.25 inches of rain fell in twenty-four hours causing the river to flood and its course to divert. These same conditions occurred again in 1942 and Edmondson's farm (shown in the photograph) was badly damaged.

Even in Wartime the Walls Fall Down

Stan Edmondson of Seathwaite Farm, Borrowdale, and his land army assistant repair the dry-stone wall bordering the road beside the farm. From here the track to Stockley Bridge, Grains Gill and Styhead Tarn commences.

"On His Shoulders Rejoicing"

A shepherd returns along the Troutbeck Valley with his lost lamb (a Wensleydale cross). Behind rise the imposing heights of Froswick, Ill Bell and Yoke.

Old Stonethwaite

Beyond Rosthwaite in Borrowdale a quiet road leads off to the left and enters the secluded hamlet of Stonethwaite. This tiny settlement, remote from modern progress, stands in peaceful solitude amidst fells of spectacular beauty.

Stonethwaite Beck flows gently through the valley over a bed of multi-coloured volcanic rock. The Elysian pools beside the footpath entice the walker to linger awhile before following the track up onto the high fells. Only in Upper Eskdale on the way to Throstle Garth are the pools rivalled by those of Stonethwaite.

Trailing at Hethersgill

The start of the hound trail at Hethersgill in North Cumberland. Hound trailing has long been a popular pastime with the inhabitants of Lakeland. The trail, sometimes as long as eight miles, is scented every quarter mile with a 'drag' steeped in aniseed which the dogs follow at breathtaking speed.

In the photograph the handlers have slipped the hounds at the start of the trail and the excitement and concentation felt by both handlers and dogs is clearly visible.

Beneath the Crags of Langstrath

The track leading from Stonethwaite in Borrowdale to the delightful upland valley of Langstrath passes beneath some of the most striking rock formations in the district - Eagle Crag (on the left of the photograph) and Bull Crag.

Here, three of the loveliest streams in Lakeland converge - Greenup Gill, Langstrath Beck and Stonethwaite Beck. Their waters, gathered from the surrounding fells, form limpid pools and graceful waterfalls, creating an area of great natural beauty.

Paths radiate from the valley over the encircling fells, guiding the walker to yet more endeavours; Greenup Edge leading to Grasmere, Stake Pass for Great Langdale and the route to Scafell Pike by Esk hause.

Grasmere Sports

A circle of amateur photographers, locals and visitors, enjoy a rare opportunity to photograph Lord Lonsdale in the enclosure at Grasmere Sports.

His Lordship had arrived earlier in his familiar fleet of yellow Rolls Royces. A small boy, equipped with a Brownie Box Camera, approached him at the finish of the Fell Race. He smiled in response to the child's eager face and immediately found himself surrounded by a group of enthusiastic photographers with their folding cameras and 'Brownies'.

Among the Skiddaw Shepherds

On 1st November, 1937 I was invited to attend the annual meet of the Skiddaw shepherds, a custom observed over many years for the purpose of restoring stray sheep to their rightful owners. The meet was held beside Black Hazel Beck near Mungrisdale, behind Blencathra, a bleak, desolate area known locally as 'Back o' Skidda'.

A number of sheep had already been assembled in a dry-stone walled enclosure while new animals steadily joined the throng. About fifty shepherds were gathered together, some with dogs and some, who had travelled from as far away as Troutbeck in Cumberland and Hesket Newmarket near Caldbeck, arrived on their sturdy fell ponies.

After a good lunch each shepherd claimed his stray sheep on payment of half a crown. Songs were sung to celebrate the gathering and an address was given.

These meets are today held in local hostelries which, although warmer and drier, lack the spirit of Black Hazel. They remain, however, a delightful memory for many.

Retaining the Old Tradition

Andrew Thompson of Hesket Newmarket near Caldbeck entertains the shepherds' meet with his rendering of 'John Peel'. The surrounding hills ring their echoes as all join in the last verse.

"From Troutbeck, Once on a Day"

One of the outstanding characters assembled for the shepherds' meet was Ned Hanson who had travelled all the way from Troutbeck in Cumberland. He arrived on a sturdy fell pony carrying a lame sheep across his saddle, escorted by a pack of sheep dogs.

Claiming Their Own

The stray sheep, assembled in the walled enclosure, are examined by the shepherds. Each was instantly recognised and claimed by its owner.

Ferry with a History

The Windermere Ferry waits for its supply of coal before making the short crossing from Ferry Nab, near Bowness Bay, to The Ferry House Hotel on the other side of the lake. Often described as 'the pleasantest spot on Windermere', the ferry passes a number of delightful islands - Belle Isle, Ladyholme, Maidenholme and Lilies of the Valley.

Over the years many legends have become associated with the ferry and one in particular still exists; a ghostly passenger, known as The Crier of Claife, calls to the boat and then haunts the ferryman to an untimely death.

Harry Lamb of Caldbeck

Harry Lamb was a much respected local farmer. His home at Greenrigg, Caldbeck formerly belonged to John Peel, the famous huntsman. His great love of the fells around his home and his flock of Herdwick sheep encouraged him to become Secretary of the Herdwick Sheep Breeders Association in 1938.

He also found time to give radio broadcasts, become a newspaper correspondent and to write. He produced 'Lamb's Shepherd's Guide' for 1937, a reference manual listing sheep markings found in Cumberland, Westmorland and North Lancashire. In the photograph he wears a jacket made of 'hodden grey' wool from his beloved Herdwick sheep.

Mary Lamb of Caldbeck

Mary Lamb of Caldbeck (Harry's daughter) achieved unexpected fame in the 1930s. She was interviewed by Collie Knox of the Daily Mail for 'In Town Tonight' and her simple philosophy and love of her rural way of life touched the imagination of many listeners.

For some time afterwards she was in great demand as a speaker, delighting her audiences with tales and anecdotes of country living.

"Grey Walls that Climb the Mountain Side, or Sink to Valleys Tender"

High above Kirkstone Pass on John Bell's Banner near Caudale Moor, two veteran dalesmen work to repair a damaged dry-stone wall. The man on the left is Mr. J. Gregg of Troutbeck in Westmorland who was well known locally for his fine singing voice.

Built mainly in the late 18th century, these sturdy survivors of an age long past march over the fells disregarding rocky outcrops and cliffs. The builders worked very long hours for small wages and often slept out on the fells to avoid the time-wasting journey back to the valley.

Some of the walls are known to be ancient; at Throstle Garth in Eskdale the foundations of a fence, probably erected by the Abbots of Furness, date back to about 1290.

Fate of Some Lakeland Predators

Fox hunting in the Lake District has been a traditional sporting activity for many generations. The season begins in early October and the huntsmen follow the hounds over the fells on foot. The fox's 'earth' is usually hidden high up on the fellside, either among rocks or on a heather or bilberry clad ledge. The fox descends to lower ground to seek food during the hours of darkness.

There are five packs of foxhounds in Lakeland - Blencathra, Eskdale and Ennerdale, Ullswater, Coniston and Melbreak - that regularly scour the heights in search of their quarry. However farmers occasionally employ a more expeditious method of safeguarding their newly-born lambs or poultry as shown in the photograph.

Gone Away

Soon after the end of the Second World War the famous Patterdale huntsman Joe 'Hunty' Bowman died and I was commissioned by Picture Post to record his funeral.

He was appointed Huntsman to the Ullswater Foxhounds in 1879 and during his career accounted for over 2,000 foxes. His considerable hunting skills were considered superior to those of the famous John Peel of Caldbeck. He retired in 1924 and several songs and books were written about him.

The photograph shows the simple funeral procession carefully making its way from his cottage in Grisedale to the graveyard in Patterdale. The coffin is carried along the stone track on a milk float.

Spring at Sizergh Castle

Three miles south of Kendal beside the A6 road stands Sizergh Castle. This ancient estate, which derives its name from old Norse meaning 'the dairy farm of Sigrid', is recorded in the Domesday Book.

The Strickland family has lived at Sizergh for over 700 years. This picture was taken in the spring of 1946 when I was asked to photograph the treasures of the castle by the late Mr. H. Hornyold-Strickland who was compiling a history of the estate and of the family.

The Summit of Kirkstone Pass

Over forty years have elapsed since this photograph of the summit of Kirkstone Pass was taken. The building on the right is the famous Kirkstone Inn (formerly called The Travellers Rest) which was reputed to be the highest inn in England.

Beyond the brow of the Pass, over the wall beneath Red Screes, stands the Kirk Stone, a boulder resembling a church tower that gave the Pass its name. In days past religious services were regularly held beside the stone.

A Perfect Blend

Travellers passing through the lovely valleys of Lakeland have long regarded the old fell farms with delight. They appear to have been born with the landscape, so well do they match their surroundings.

Birkhowe nestles contentedly in the unspoilt valley of Little Langdale encompassed by its guardian mountains - Wetherlam, Lingmoor and Blake Rigg. Nearby is picturesque Little Langdale Tarn. Birkhowe, in common with many of Lakeland's farms, is under the ownership of The National Trust which protects and preserves these fine examples of traditional architecture for future generations of travellers to enjoy.

Freewheeling in Borrowdale

A group of five young ladies enjoying the tranquillity of traffic-free roads as they cycle towards Seathwaite at the head of Borrowdale.

The spring sunshine on the steep flanks of Base Brown seems to light up the whole valley that so often is sombre and heavy with mist and rain clouds.

To the left is Seathwaite Fell and the 'Stee' leading to Sty Head and England's highest peaks; to the right is the hanging valley of Gillercombe and the falls of Sour Milk Gill.

At a Westmorland Farm Sale

A friendly word from a member of Kendal Borough Police to Joseph Nicholson of Lamb Howe, Winster, aged 84, at a farm sale in Westmorland. These occasions were attended by many of the local farmers who enjoyed the rare opportunity of a leisurely chat with their neighbours.

The Fell Ponies of Mickleden

The beautiful wild ponies of Mickleden are a sight enjoyed by fellwalkers as they pass through the head of Great Langdale. These sturdy beasts persistently greet visitors hoping perhaps to persuade them to part with a morsel of their carefully-packed picnic. Although the Mickleden ponies are the best known, other groups also exist throughout Lakeland as far as the Howgill Fells.

Centuries ago wild ponies were present all over England. Farmers tended to cross them with domesticated horses in an attempt to produce a larger animal for use on the farm. Eventually a National Trust Stud was established in the late 1930s mainly through the generosity of Mr. R.B. Charlton who presented three mares to the Trust. The descendants of these mares can be seen wandering on Gowbarrow Fell, Ullswater.

Evening Storm Clouds over Langdale

Fletcher Buntin and his sister Hannah of Robinson Place, Great Langdale hurry to bring in the last load of hay as storm clouds threaten from the north west. A brief glimpse of the westering sun over the Pikes creates a dramatic atmosphere in this much loved valley.

The Way to the High Fells

Middlefell is a typical Lakeland farm and stands at the head of Great Langdale beside the track leading to Mickleden. From here walkers begin their ascent to Scafell, Great Gable and the Passes of Stake and Esk Hause.

The farm is owned by The National Trust and the photograph shows one of the tenants, Mr. J. Youdell, with his flock of Herdwick sheep, brought down from the fells for lambing.

High Summer at the Head of Great Langdale

A fine amphitheatre of fells guarding the valley head surrounds this busy scene, farmers and visitors together enjoying the timeless tradition of haymaking.

The fells in the background are familiar to generations of walkers; Kettle Crag, Pike o' Blisco, Great Knott, Crinkle Crags, Shelter Crags and The Band leading to Bowfell.

A Rescue High on the Langdales

The end of January 1934 saw a drama of heroic proportions. Three Lakeland terriers, Spider, Set and Floss, were sent down a 'strong borran' on Sergeant Man after a fox which had been persued to ground by the Coniston Foxhounds.

The terriers became trapped and a rescue operation was mounted under the leadership of Braithwaite Black of Ambleside, a local hunter and dog breeder. Many willing volunteers offered their services but after nine days of fruitless effort Mr. Black was eventually lowered into the borran by a rope tied to his feet.

One dog, Spider, was secured, very little the worse for its ordeal, but unfortunately the other two dogs perished after sustained efforts for a further three days failed to retrieve them. The photograph shows Harry Mounsey holding Spider, Arthur Askew or 'Chippy' Pierce, Bill Wood, Bob Birkett and Gordon Robinson gently lifting the little dog to safety.

Lambing Time at Hartsop Hall

After climbing 'The Struggle' out of Ambleside to the summit of the Kirkstone Pass, the traveller descends through the strath of Kirkstonefoot to reach Brothers Water. This pretty stretch of water, attracting both wildfowl and fishermen, derives its name from an unfortunate accident that occurred in December 1785 when two young brothers were drowned after falling through thin ice.

The photograph shows John Allen of Hartsop Hall surveying some of his Swaledale ewes and their lambs.

The Rewarding Toil of Manual Harvesting

St. Mary's Church, Crosthwaite, towering above the surrounding countryside, benignly surveys the annual wheat harvest. In the photograph Billy Inman of Crosthwaite Mill Farm and Jack Wilson of Long Green Farm patiently wait for the remaining two sheaves of wheat to complete the stook.

The church, restored during the last century, contains a font presented to the parish by the restorers. A note displayed on the wall tells of a bequest made 200 years ago whereby 2s. 6d. was to be paid annually for whipping dogs out of the church.

When Helsington Had a School

Playtime in the little village school of Helsington, near Kendal. The school and the pretty 18th century church stand on a spur of Scout Scar, high above the broad, lush Lyth Valley - "a stretch of green silk shot with buttercup gold".

To the left of the children is Mrs. Whillan the headmistress, a delightful lady who was loved by all who knew her.

Tree Felling at Blea Tarn

The magnificence of Blea Tarn (blea means blue) lying between the valleys of Great and Little Langdale, is temporarily spoiled by timber felling beside its edge. These fine straight pines were used by Coniston and Langdale quarries for a variety of purposes including quarry ladders.

The setting of Blea Tarn is considered by many to be the most beautiful in Lakeland. Wordsworth's "lusty twins", the famous Langdale Pikes, provide a background of grandeur to this rural scene.

In springtime the footpath from the tarn to Fell Foot near Wrynose Pass is edged with a profusion of bog myrtle whose fragrance fills the surrounding air.

Artists in Stone

Alan and Jimmy Jackson of The Row Farm in the Lyth Valley expertly demonstrate the ancient art of dry stone walling. Most of the Lakeland dry-stone walls were originally constructed between the middle of the 18th century and the middle of the 19th century following the General Enclosures Act of 1801. These impressive structures, so often the only companions of hardy fellwalkers, require constant maintenance to prevent livestock from straying and to provide some shelter for the sheep high on the fells.

Worth Fighting For

Spring 1946, the end of the Second World War, and the damson blossom in the Lyth Valley near Kendal was resplendent, almost as a thanksgiving. William Walling of Dawson Fold, Crosthwaite was in his eighties when he told me that he had never seen a finer display.

Picture Post published this photograph and a close friend who saw the picture pinned to the notice board in the Naafi Canteen in Rangoon wrote to say how homesick it made him feel.

"Is My Team Ploughing?"

A.E. Houseman's 'Shropshire Lad' is recalled in this rural scene. Two magnificent horses in splendid condition and aged respectively twenty-seven and twenty-eight years, pull the plough for Mr. W. Milburn of Crook.

Sheep Wash Bridge

This picturesque bridge lies a few hundred yards from the Underbarrow to Crosthwaite road. It fords Underbarrow Beck at Low Grighall and is officially called Ellers Bridge. However, the older farmers of the area know it simply as Sheep Wash Bridge because of the deep pool on its south side that was regularly used for washing sheep.

The farmer in the picture is taking his faulty plough to be repaired at the Crosthwaite smithy.

A Dying Art

Craftmanship is displayed in every line of this picture as the elderly farmer inspects the corn stack that he is in the process of building. The safe placing of the ladder and the fine lines of supporting wires display a sense of correctness which is rarely noticeable in today's modern methods.

The Farmer's in the Pub

Two well trained sheepdogs keep order while their master enjoys his break in the Sun Inn at Crook, near Kendal.

Craftsmen of Crosthwaite

Crosthwaite village smithy, a landmark for many years, still stands to remind us of days gone by. These fine working horses have been taken to the smithy for reshoeing by Joe Taylor and George Stewardson.

Feathering

Sally Inman of Draw Well Farm, The How, in the Lyth Valley near Kendal, busily cuts the stubs off hens' feathers in preparation for making pillows.

Sheep Dipping Time

A high-lying valley deep in the Westmorland fells provides the location for one of the periodic local sheep washings.

The beck has been dammed to form a pool into which the sheep are unceremoniously flung from the bank. The sheep ably swim through the water to the opposite bank thereby cleansing their fleeces before shearing.

Lakeland Yeomen

George and James Walling of Dawson Fold near Crosthwaite, Westmorland, represent a standard of yeoman farmer who built up an impressive reputation for farming in this area in the middle years of this century.

The Language of Flowers

A kindly neighbour, Mrs. Nelson of Rose Cottage, Linstock, near Carlisle, presents my $2^{1}/_{2}$ year old son with flowers from her garden to console him for sustaining a poisoned hand. Her 'cloutie' bonnet, a traditional Lakeland design made from large scraps of cotton, was generally worn during haymaking to protect the face and neck from the hot sun.

The photograph was taken in the summer of 1937 when her lovely garden was in full bloom.

Near the Source of the River Kent

Jack Fishwick drives his flock of Swaledale sheep back onto the fells after clipping at Hartrigg Farm.

In the background stand the magnificent fells that encircle the head of Kentmere and surround Hall Gill, the source of the delightful River Kent.

"Whither Now". Armistice Day, November 1932

A young boy and his dog stand at Waterside, Kendal gazing through the misty brightness at the hurrying waters of the River Kent.

An abandoned tank, a relic of the First World War, grimly surveys the river from Miller Field, a vivid reminder of the horrors so recently witnessed and a portent of events yet to come.